'Donald Moss returns with a ne
his extraordinary ability to listei
Rivers of words have been written on the effects of COVID-19
on clinical work. We then need to distance ourselves from all
this noise. *Psychoanalysis in a Plague Year* offers us this possibility. Not theories, concepts, abstractions; instead, the event,
every time new and daily, lived many times but always amazing:
the spoken word and the experience of a special space in which
to welcome it. With delicacy, discretion and a fine sense of
humor, Donald Moss brilliantly captures the essence of psychoanalysis in a dimension that is not purely cognitive, but also,
and perhaps primarily, poetic-aesthetic, sensory and bodily.'

Giuseppe Civitarese *is author of* Sublime
Subjects: Aesthetic Experience and Intersubjectivity
in Psychoanalysis *(2017)*

'The reality of COVID-19 is present here not in the reported
statements but in the shape they make on the page, and the time
(the timing) those shapes suggest. Many of the days' notations,
looked at together, seem like negative sonnets, or lines on their
way toward the full fourteen and not quite getting there. They
are sonnets of negation, but so are most sonnets. How rare it is,
whatever the surrounding calm of supporting belief, for verse
to have happiness happen on the page or in the prosody—or
even, if happiness is too much (the wrong thing) to ask for, then
simply the feeling of things taking a turn for the better.
Moments like these occur in the book, but they are rare. I think
that is because they are rare in poetry in general.'

Timothy J. Clark *is Professor Emeritus of the History of Art at
the University of California, Berkeley. His most recent books
are* Picasso and Truth: From Cubism to Guernica *(2013) and*
Heaven on Earth: Patining and the Life to Come *(2018)*

PSYCHOANALYSIS IN A PLAGUE YEAR

Selecting one sentence from each session every day, Donald Moss has recorded the words spoken by his patients during one year of 'Covid-time'. The patients conjure a moving mixture of the mundane and extraordinary, giving readers a perspective on psychoanalytic practice and treatment during the COVID-19 pandemic.

Clustered together in ways akin to poetic verse, these sentences preserve the mood of the analyst's working day, reflecting the common ground shared by analyst and patient in these unprecedented times. Pandemic-related concerns and everyday problems are seen to persist in these extreme circumstances, affording the reader clinical insights into the daily life of contemporary psychoanalysts. With a clear preface from the author and a remarkable foreword by Timothy J. Clark, the book is grounded in a contemporary psychoanalytic context.

An insightful companion into psychoanalytic practice, the book will interest therapists and analysts in training and in practice, as well as readers intrigued by what happens behind the closed doors of the consulting room.

Donald Moss has been a psychoanalyst in New York for 40 years and was most recently the recipient of the Haskell Norman Prize for excellence in psychoanalysis (2020). He is part of the College Executive of the *International Journal of Psychoanalysis*, a member of the Holmes Commission on Racial Equality in the American Psychoanalytic Association, and a founding member of the Green Gang.

PSYCHOANALYSIS IN A PLAGUE YEAR

Donald Moss

Routledge
Taylor & Francis Group

LONDON AND NEW YORK

Cover image: © Artwork by Nicholas Garland

First published 2023
by Routledge
4 Park Square, Milton Park, Abingdon, Oxon OX14 4RN

and by Routledge
605 Third Avenue, New York, NY 10158

Routledge is an imprint of the Taylor & Francis Group, an informa business

British Library Cataloguing-in-Publication Data
A catalogue record for this book is available from the British Library

Library of Congress Cataloging-in-Publication Data
Names: Moss, Donald, 1949- author.
Title: Psychoanalysis in a plague year / Donald Moss.
Description: Milton Park, Abingdon, Oxon; New York, NY: Routledge, 2022.
Identifiers: LCCN 2021062112 (print) | LCCN 2021062113 (ebook) | ISBN 9781032207599 (hardback) | ISBN 9781032207605 (paperback) | ISBN 9781003265092 (ebook)
Subjects: LCSH: Psychotherapist and patient. | COVID-19 (Disease)—Psychological aspects.
Classification: LCC RC480.8 .M673 2022 (print) | LCC RC480.8 (ebook) | DDC 616.89/14—dc23/eng/20211224
LC record available at https://lccn.loc.gov/2021062112
LC ebook record available at https://lccn.loc.gov/2021062113

ISBN: 9781032207599 (hbk)
ISBN: 9781032207605 (pbk)
ISBN: 9781003265092 (ebk)

DOI: 10.4324/9781003265092

Typeset in Times New Roman
by KnowledgeWorks Global Ltd.

I dedicate this book to my wife Lynne and to my children Hannah, Ivan, and Isaiah.

PREFACE

In March 2020, I fled New York. For most of the next year my partner and I lived in a house in the woods. I saw almost nobody. I conducted my life and my practice exclusively by phone and computer.

The woods are beautiful. As never before, I felt I could see them; could be a participant in the forest's lives. Coyotes, owls, frogs, a fox—I was one of the animals. Like them, I would live for a while and then die. Mortality seemed fair, a simple condition affecting all of us.

But of course I was also not one of the animals. I was here involuntarily, arrested. The space permitted me was surrounded by a deadly perimeter. Outside that perimeter every person posed a threat.

The woods were both refuge and enclosure. This set-up was an inversion. The tables had turned. I was safe only away from civilization.

I tried to make sense of it all, to find precedents, look for similarities: maybe a wartime narrative, people running from bombs, from urban terror. This narrative didn't work, though. Coronavirus was not a bomb. There was no enemy, no invasion.

No one did this—no deed, no error, no slipup. A balance has been disturbed, a separation compromised. Humans had weakened a wall. A tiny thing had breached it.

* * *

After each session in the woods, I chose a sentence. To make the choice, I tried to change my customary mind-set from listening to overhearing. Clinical listening, I thought, is work—informed by aim, purpose, and aspiration. But overhearing is effortless—devoid of intention, grounded in accident and serendipity.

With this project, I wanted the impossible: to strip myself of purpose and the sentences of context. I wanted to ask no questions, to take the first step in an act of associative recollection and to stop there, to take no second step. Extract one sentence at a time, leave it where it lay, then link up the sentences, collate them into a daily verse.

Waiting for a train, say, you overhear things—snippets—and you turn those snippets into information. You sense a buzz. These sentences are like that, a buzz, overheard on a psychoanalytic platform.

I also kept a journal.

Two dreams from the first night:

1   A punk in a sports car drives up, playing Dixie or some other song of the Confederacy, playing it loudly. I tell him he can't do that, play that kind of racist music. He slams on the brakes, jumps out of his car and confronts me, nose-to-nose. I don't back down. You can't play that music. It's racist. You haven't the right. I explain it to him and he listens. He quiets down. He will turn off the music. I'm surprised. Reason has actually been effective.

2   I am with Christian and his father. They are showing me a special part of a special river. It's in a cave, far away and difficult to access, a secret cave. The water is particularly deep and in its depths are large perfect beautiful trout. I am doubly happy— that there is such a place supporting such trout, that Christian and his father know of it, and that they've told me/shown me. Large perfect beautiful trout in a deep place.

Living here, having had to flee New York, this is what I need access to: effective reason and large perfect beautiful trout living in a deep place.

Deprived of my city, my surround, my people, my machines, my streets, I have to call upon myself, and my beloveds, in ways I never have had to. These two dreams mark hope, maybe I can find what I need to find.

These sentences, then, my trout; this project, then, my reason.

FOREWORD

"I don't have the right to speak about myself to you" (Day 103).

What mattered most to me in the following pages—I realized this a few hours after finishing them, and it seemed a revelation—was the sound of human distress. "I don't know how to get out there with you" (Day 86). "Harder, harder, closer, don't forgive—that's you Dr. Conscience" (Day 124). "That's how I would be if I were alive" (Day 170). That distress is entangled with absurdity and self-indulgence does not alter things. Since when, with humanity, has it not been? The depth of distress is dreadful, horrible—all the more so for the accompanying comedy. "Eight hours of Twitter since yesterday's session" (Day 171). "Would that have been doing something?" (Day 17). "I think you're gardening while we speak" (Day 65).

Why is it that we human animals are so unhappy—still as angry and inconsolable as one-year-olds—in spite of our satisfied wants, privileges, powers and distractions, the love and loyalty of others? "I am becalmed by applause" (Day 70). "I'm moved by you but then what?" (Day 93). "I can't stand the word 'love'" (Day 96). Psychoanalysis, as I understand it, is—remains—an attempt to answer that question. Any culture that does not wish, or is not able, to pose it (or recognize that it is a question) will end, I am sure .... Well, nowhere good.

"Dr. Moss has become impatient with me" (Day 165). "You exhaled as though in pain" (Day 14). "You're too much of a communist to get this" (Day 105). I hope that up in the Zoom corner at such moments was the face of the Dr. Moss I know, grinning at the whole unlikelihood of being.

Reading the book again, I'm aware that extracting single sentences from the matrix, though I couldn't resist it the first time through, does violence to the book's poetry—to the lack of story it wants to tell. The reality of COVID-19 is present here not in the reported statements but in the shape they make on the page, and the time (the timing) those shapes suggest. Many of the days' notations, looked at together, seem like negative sonnets, or lines on their way toward the full fourteen and not quite getting there. They are sonnets of negation, but so are most sonnets. ("My mistress' eyes are nothing like the sun.") How rare it is, whatever the surrounding calm or supporting belief, for verse to have *happiness* happen on the page or in the prosody—or even, if happiness is too much (the wrong thing) to ask for, then simply the feeling of things taking a turn for the better. "Now I understand myself more fully." "Therefore I forgive you." "I can feel my body softening when you speak" (Day 177). "I want to thank you for your advice" (Day 85). Moments like these occur in the book, but they are rare. I think that is because they are rare in poetry in general. The kinds of speech acts just listed, one or two of them my inventions, are things (wonders) I associate with the great nineteenth-century novelists ... Tolstoy, George Eliot. Out of them came Freud.

"I don't have the right to speak about myself to you": that entry sticks sadly in the mind. What can it be that denies a person such a right, and what might give it back? That's the question I hear in these pages—it seems another way of putting the question of psychoanalysis with which I began. I fumble for a way to put it more clearly. That's because the question, or any question much like it, is put less and less often in the life we're given, because our culture believes it needn't be—shouldn't be. The right to speak about myself to someone else—about myself, not my selfie ... to speak, not to parrot someone else's identity declaration ... How could a culture like ours accommodate such a right? (Speaking would get in the way of spending. Self would put "individuality" in doubt.) But without such a right a culture is nothing.

Timothy J. Clark

DAY 1

Did you forget you could kill yourself?
What if she slept with this other guy?
Yesterday the salad, today the cookie.
I live for the constant alarm, the 24/7.
Then I switched to Armenian chants.
Aren't you saying that it's wrong?
It's what I did, and guess still do, sometimes …
My phone gives me a weekly update.
Shut the fuck up and give me the baby.
All I ask is for one Friday night dinner.
We deserved this a long time ago.

DAY 2

I picture their kiss and everything else.
Young men are spitting on the street.
We're not really meeting—that's the problem.
When I had the bedbugs, he absolutely freaked out.
I am the tree, she is the boy.
When we're done, it won't be on me.
What is this notion of irreducible?
Six minutes late and I sound like an idiot.
But …
In some ways, it was quite innocuous.
This is an emergency.

DOI: 10.4324/9781003265092-1

DAY 3

You're insane.
It's not my fault that she's alone.
I'm just trying to keep my sanity.
And I got attacked by a bunch of ants.
What I feel is just tired.
You're the only one here.
It's tawdry to talk with you.
I want help.
How long can I go without seeing a human?
For me, shelter in place is great.

DAY 4

I'll be better when the sun comes in.
There's a bit more of a human.
I was just looking for some comfort.
It wasn't really your idea anyway.
What I'm doing is suspect, isn't it?
Online contact is a fragile reminder.
Sorry for the crossed emails.
I have no idea what's coming out of my mouth.
My mother feels that way.

DAY 5

Wash your hands; say please and thank you.
Everybody's going a bit insane.
He's diligent and I'm by myself.
My hand is bleeding so now they'll love me.
I have good quality headphones.
I'll leave you on your ass with nothing.
Where'd you find the balls for that?
The world doesn't affect me very much.
You and me have approached that at times, I think.
It was the most blissful experience I've had.

DAY 6

Who do you think you are?
I'm wound a little tight, I guess.
Do you know anyone yet who's died?
At least I'm not ignoring my kids.
This is something grave and bad.
I pretend to preserve a pretended peace.
If you don't do, you don't get.
Where might dating life be heading?
I think there's a levelling going on.

DAY 7

"I want" is not really me wanting.
When I think, it's just me going blank.
A woman mechanic—she was so hot.
What do they see in me, anyway?
I always find my way to injury.
You can probably hear the panic in my voice.
It's beautiful here and maybe there too.
I only want to be quiet and alone.
It's time for birdsong and humansong.

DAY 8

Where is your compassion?
He seems cheap and slimy.
OK, I think we should meet.
I maybe scoffed a little at first.
But they should just open a can of beans.
Everyone was fighting for my soul.
Community transmission, I'll call it.
I'm wasting the time we're given.
With us two, it's support gone bad.
There's never normal with my mother.

DAY 9

This house is in foreclosure.
Reality always jars me.
I can't get away with it.
I need to be activated by someone else.
It's a bit of a dire situation.
Someone drank the Kool-Aid.
But I don't know where to go from here.
Lo and Behold, I just got inspired.
I want to be the wise charismatic leader.
You and me, let's do it.

DAY 10

Quarantine is a gift.
It's her stubborn Southern paranoia.
I'm more lonely than ever.
We have, like, one nice scene.
I had a good session with my baby niece.
Pretending, that was the word we used.
I found some kind of happiness, connection.
How do I remake myself?
I wanted to touch her back, touch anyone.

DAY 11

I don't have any real criminal impulse.
I'm watching her slowly die.
Can I call you later?
I have a fucking wasp in my eye.
I want younger, newer.
It shook my feeling of immortality.
I want to get off the phone and die.
I'm stuck in getting older.
The virus and the tics both upset her.
I need to help others now.

DAY 12

I feel like I'm in danger.
I could have slaughtered him.
It's not a great pairing with my psyche.
There's a plausible scenario where I end up dead.
And now I have even less to say.
Will I still be who I was?
I am groping for some form of method.
Has the price of cocaine gone up or down?
We'll just be nice and do that together.
I wish that I had more.

DAY 13

I want a working interior.
I may not be capable of self-reflection.
It annoys me that she's ordering dolls.
I withdraw from you and your ugly truths.
Death is much more approachable now.
The virus is a really advanced wise thing.
I know, I know, I know.
It's the all-around control, the busybodies.
I live in a shell of distraction.
She's flipped her lid with the kids.
Do I have to talk with you?
I sense myself becoming my dad.

DAY 14

You exhaled as though in pain.
I don't feel crazy for wondering.
Just make a fucking decision, why don't you.
I'd like to kind of put boundaries on it.
You ask me to poke a stick in a fresh wound.
It's simple but it's doomed.
I'm yelling at the kids like an animal.
I can't come up with an answer to anything.
I want being in the world again.

DAY 15

I need to be everything.
I need to cancel our appointment.
I'm not superior; those people are just animals.
I am not doing well.
I can never get it right.
I have nothing, nothing, ever, to say to you.
So I won't say anything then.
My capacity for discernment sets me apart.
Both of our cats died in the fire.
I can't change what needs to change.

DAY 16

I can't interpret the world.
Don't get hung up on the language thing.
I dreamt you used to be a woman.
I don't want to give you a blow by blow.
My being always disappoints him.
My parents had no clue.
I know you didn't mean it that way.
Whereas Sunday was so charming.
I don't want her to feel misshapen.

DAY 17

This is not a way to be.
I don't know the difference between a dove and a pigeon.
I've never been in better shape.
It works for me but for no one else.
Good, I mean fine, I guess.
There are rabbits on my favorite hill.
That is devastating.
Would that have been doing something?
It was so clear just yesterday.
None of this stuff is playing video games.

DAY 18

I felt mutilated when my father died.
My thoughts are on the edge of paranoid.
We have a psychopath on our hands.
"Dr. Moss" assumes the role of a tyrant.
Whatever you say is absolute.
Everything is taken care of.
I keep saying I'm sorry but never mean it.
I try for an ambiguous identity.

DAY 19

It all stopped when I was 20.
I was so sad when she left.
How are you faring in all of this?
I don't like the sound of what you're saying.
You're such a fucking bulldozer.
I feel abandoned and unsafe.
That's fine, since I'll die soon anyway.
You feel confident enough to send me into the world?
OK, so have a session, migraine or not.

DAY 20

You just pop in and out as you like.
I just wanted to take a bike ride.
I'm a flawed dad and he's a flawed son.
No offense, but I think it's a male thing.
And it's my birthday tomorrow.
She must not lose her mind.
Why do I live like this?
I'm just trying to make sense of it.
Yesterday, then today—something good is going on.
For the first time, I can imagine having children.

DAY 21

This call is my only point of continuity.
I want these appointments to be important.
I'm about to have a breakdown.
I am not in solitary confinement.
What if I'm injured and don't die?
You don't feel dangerous when you're exasperated.
I hosted a Zoom memorial service for my dad.
What's really wrong with me?
I want to die.
I was debating whether to call you at all.

DAY 22

You would cringe, if you knew I'd said that.
Why am I the only adult in the room here?
Let's hope it stays that way.
Everything I say is a lie.
It's not really living.
My mom and I save each other from dying.
Thank you for accommodating my needs.
Are we infecting our kids?
I am so ashamed.
You're just a bad object.

DAY 23

I have to remain in this humble state.
You're fucking retarded.
Please stop saying I'm dead.
This is going to be the rest of my life.
I am not the problem.
He's able to say exactly the wrong thing.
I don't want to be anywhere else on the planet.
The continuity of a healthy mindset is valuable.
That's exactly what I think.

DAY 24

She married a very wealthy man.
I want to get a lot of house plants.
You're not even worthy of cleaning my ass.
I don't know the work of persuasion.
I don't say that with resentment.
And he loved that boat.
Are you ever going back to Manhattan?
I am automatically someone's slave.
Can you hear that fly?
She got pregnant.

DAY 25

They just don't stand a chance.
I don't want to grind it out.
You think it might not be constitutional?
Don't do stupid shit.
If they need me, they'll love me.
She's very much into re-use.
I don't know how to think.
It's my fate, just like my sisters.
I told her about my relapse.
My fury management system is gone.
My baby is a timekeeper.

DAY 26

And of course I think of you.
I don't have a Plan B.
It's partly therapy but the kids are getting older.
I feel unsettled by relaxation.
I can and I have to.
I move forward to get nowhere.
I should make a fucking list.
Why did she have to be actually crazy?
It's only fair.
That's all I have to say.

DAY 27

She'll only say I'm a monster.
She's definitely in a high-risk category.
You can't talk to Moss about that.
I want compassion from you.
He's the ruler of the universe.
It was beautiful but I didn't fit in.
Maybe you should go.
I sound like a dick.
I will be disappointed if she doesn't want to be abused.
You were thoughtless too.

DAY 28

It's real and it's not my doing.
That's all the relatively normal news.
I don't feel like it's a betrayal.
I'm the object of their judgments.
It's sad to have to be so cagey.
This is a bunch of nonsense.
And it sucks.
I struggle with expressing anger.
I'm very happy with you on the phone.
Here's a visual.
Why can't I just feel normal?

DAY 29

I have all my materials here.
And of course I feel vindicated.
I am overshadowed by worry.
Everything you say is right.
Trauma creates emotional memories.
My dad and I hadn't communicated.
Maybe that whale will come back.
I'm a real person talking to you.
I have a perfect desk in a private room.
I had a full day today.

DAY 30

That's a much better way of putting it.
It's a good feeling when it works.
Why are you giving him all the benefits?
Something scares me about freedom.
I'm back to where I started.
You're better than me.
Help me out here, Dr. Moss.
I'm on another call.
Are you interested in dreams?

DAY 31

I want the painless natural outcome.
I used to be, like, very hopeful.
My life is not servile or slavish.
If I hurt her, she'll see what she's missing.
This may be the end.
I don't want to do the real work anymore.
I want to empower people, not shame them.
What I did was three hours of video and twitter.
Let the record show that I called.
When's your birthday?

DAY 32

That's not what you're supposed to do.
It's not like I'm speaking Chinese here.
Bye, Don.
NY is an absolute shameful disgrace.
They never tell me anything.
I apologize for the calls last week.
You are just another task.
I identified always with my mom.
I don't know if I'm living life right.

DAY 33

I was something that happened to them.
I'll translate and read the whole thing to you.
You don't know that.
I have a bit of a dilemma.
I can't satisfy my wife.
Each moment is an inflection point.
He asks me to play when I'm already playing.
I walk the woods on the periphery.
I can't be disingenuous.

DAY 34

You see me as shallow.
It touches me and puts me at peace.
The belt buckle flayed my back.
Why won't you protect me?
I don't know how to push.
The thing I saw was so sure.
My life is finished.
How are they this flat?

DAY 35

I realize I don't have infinite time.
We have no life of our own here.
I want something that no longer exists.
It didn't have a restorative effect.
Don't I feel that I have worth?
I don't want to be more by myself.
He's gonna own the fucking game.
I'm overstepping some sort of boundary.
I'm in an excellent mood.

DAY 36

She's probably envious of me.
This would be heaven.
I got her to relent a little bit.
I'm not the big man she wants.
It's the goal-scoring I crave.
All this crap comes up on my computer.
My mother wants nothing to do with me.
I'm ready for a big argument with you.
I don't want to be your confidante.
I'm like Mr. Potato-Head.
She almost died of a shortage of something.

DAY 37

The task is to be charming.
Sorry for being so weirdly scattered today.
Why sign on to be such a shit?
The consequences are scary.
I have hairy arms like my dad did.
Everyone's figured it out but me.
It's difficult to communicate a feeling.
I'm just talking to talk.
I want a religious experience.
I want you to be thoughtful and eloquent.

DAY 38

Have you experienced what I just described?
Nothing can satisfy this appetite.
I can't do it for even one sentence.
Why does everyone want to fuck me?
I could stay in my prison forever.
Someone's always watching me.
It's not a super happy cry.
Don't put that on me.

DAY 39

Have you noticed a newly emerging psychology?
I can't remember ever asking a favor.
I sat in the garden all day.
I've totally stopped drinking.
I can't control anything.
I would have been a monastic.
I'm an unemployed angry man.
Politics are absent.
You underestimate your power.

DAY 40

First I'm in, then I'm out.
Nothing will have happened.
Fuck you, mom.
Do I mourn for who I was?
I'm embarrassed to be in this country.
I can't talk today.
I would rather freeze than do anything.
Prada doesn't give a fuck.
Everything is evaporating very fast.
Why can't someone take care of me?
This is an eating disorder.

DAY 41

I can't engage with all of this.
I'm terrified of being seen naked.
I'm not trying to say anything, again.
I'm slowing down, thinking.
Is it mystical or is it crazy?
I infect everyone around me.
Maybe the violence has peaked.
I had a real fear of failing out.
I hate when you end on time.

DAY 60 (SOME DAYS LOST TO COMPUTER GLITCH)

If I go outside, I'll die alone.
I used to lose and now I'm losing worse.
Something about leaving makes me sad.
Shall we have sex?
You're a god, you're a god.
What you said is worth considering.
I reduced myself to an adolescent.
The looting high is like a drug high.
You mean a Satanic thing?
I want there to be meaning.

DAY 61

There is no place for me on the planet.
I believe in perfection.
Nothing comes to me.
I need no help with my judgement.
I want my insides entirely scooped out.
It was all stupid and crazy men.
I'm all over the place.
Reality is just another way of seeing nothing.
The rhythm is there and then it's gone.
I don't want my son to see me like that.

DAY 62

I am cursed.
I got scolded three times yesterday.
I wanted to make sure I didn't fuck up.
I'm angry at him and better than him.
I came to hate sports.
I am ashamed to be the father in this family.
That brutal voice is the hammer.
I will ruin this friendship.

DAY 63

No matter where I go, I'm still there.
I assign my anxiety to things or whatever.
I'm watching a lot of junk TV these days.
Thinking of particulars might be a place to start.
I don't feel well.
I understand but then I don't.
I'm disputatious and self-centered.
I have the zealotry of the convert.

DAY 64

I want someone to think for me.
I'm not doing the right thing with you.
I can't deny that it's really gotten to me.
Crazy's not the word for it.
He genuinely loves everybody in the family.
She's not fit to carry my bags.
I'm frustrated and volatile.
It's like this feeling of fear.

DAY 65

You're tactful because I'm so fragile.
I want to see my mother and sister.
I have this appointment with you.
He is not God.
You fat, lazy piece of shit.
I want you to fix it.
I think you're gardening while we speak.
They only have each other.
There's an instantaneous detachment.
I love the purity of hitting a golf ball.

DAY 66

I have to stop needing affirmation.
We washed it down with two bottles of wine.
How's the rest of your life going?
She's talking about her pregnancies at the funeral.
I got comfortable with these one night stands.
Zombies come after me each time.
It's been a really rough week.

DAY 70

Please don't abuse me.
How do I live with myself?
So I can seduce attractive women.
I want to try more things.
I felt I had ruined my life.
I'm listening to the tone of voice.

DAY 71

There's no evading scorn.
There's online access on the boat.
No one ever spoke in my family.
Do you have tips for me?
I enjoy telling you about people.
Do you think I'm depressed?
We have so much on the table.
She's dumping shit on my head.
I need somebody with experience.

DAY 72

I'm not really an actor-outer.
My adversary is a liar and a bully.
Nine out of ten you'll get it wrong.
Don't be so hard on yourself, Daddy.
I am becalmed by applause.
My dear friend just passed away.
What you said just blew my mind.

DAY 73

If someone would only read me my rights.
Can't means you've tried and failed.
I've never brought welts to my back.
I can't keep living like this.
I view him, like, he's my dad.
I could spend serious time with this person.
It doesn't literally come from books.

DAY 74

A huge amount of time goes into seducing women.
These knives make chopping a visceral pleasure.
You're just so fat.
You won't connect with me, really.
I just want to see God.
I can't let myself off the hook.
Help me out here, Dr. Moss
Is it true or is it a memory?
These are totally uninvited guests.

DAY 75

Maybe there was a little bit of terror.
If I have to pay, I'll pay.
I don't want to talk to you today; goodbye.
The window was made of triangles pointing in.
I'm so pathetic.
My dogs are too shrill.
I'll take care of Mom, don't worry.
Had I the choice, I wouldn't have been born.
We get yelled at whenever we're professional.

DAY 76

It's bizarre that I live without sex.
I was a freak then and a freak now.
That's why I'm trying to talk about it.
I fit in with weird loser psychos.
Can you see and hear me?
Maybe this is a tipping point.
There's a weight on my chest and a pit in my stomach.

DAY 77

Do I look like someone with a castration complex?
I want to be seen as a real man.
Yes, I do look down on them.
It was either murder or euthanasia.
I don't know if I'm a happy or unhappy person.
I don't know if I ever felt safe.
It's such an interesting activity—it turns off my mind completely.
Standing still is the only way to really manage.
Sex is such a simple pleasure.
There's something wrong with how I was talking yesterday.

DAY 78

My advisors are against it.
I'm brought up short by you asking that question.
I'm self-conscious that what I'm saying is bullshit.
I definitely cannot be my own psychotherapist.

DAY 79

You just really have to figure out what I want.
Wanting to be closer is unrealistic and not what you do.
You're really ugly when you act like this.
I reject the idea of distrusting people.
I only know what I don't want to feel.
I have no earthly idea why they invited me in.
I'm drawn to sources of care.

DAY 80

Why is it so dark here and so light there?
Don't even think about having a better life.
I feel electrified or, better yet, electrocuted.
Maybe I should accept money from my mother.
The constraints imposed are not light.
It's partly due to this little woman from Texas.
Maybe I feel disconnected from all the news.
My son is like me.
I am owned.

DAY 81

I have nothing of value to say.
I don't look forward to anything.
I don't let a day go by without doing something, usually
eating.
There were two metros, a bus and still a chunk of forest.
What is the actual issue about racism?
Now what?
I want to get in your head and know if you like me.
This is a sexual bacchanal beyond imagination.
I really didn't want to stop.

DAY 82

Irreversibility terrifies me.
I want them asking just who is this guy.
I don't live in real time.
It might just be that I'm waking up.
I'm so pathetic.
I'm afraid you will scold me.
The forest is tangled, tangled, tangled, and really dirty.
They take my money and fuck me up.
It's a radical strategy—honesty.

DAY 83

Who is this entitled little prick?
I will so miss my daughter.
Please don't talk to me like that.
You say I'm not depressed, just lonely.
I display the same kind of cruelty that they did.
Where I am in this isn't worth your thought.
It's standard stuff, isn't it, my wanting you to like me?
I have to see a peaceful end point.
What you said is worth exploring.
If you have any advice on this, I'm all ears.

DAY 84

It's glamor and fairy dust I'm after.
There's never a break from responsibility.
You're fucking freaking me out: I'm sorry.
How do I tell it's me you care about?
You can tell your colleagues what a piece of shit I am.
They'll presume I've cheated on my wife.
That was my mother just now.
If only there had been a trauma.
I'm picking my skin, reading a little, picking things up—I
like it.
I'm not like the other trust fund babies.
My wife is a wall.

DAY 85

I'm not content but I do accept it.
With you, it's more intellectual than experiential.
I can't identify with you.
You say it's real but I don't really know.
I may want to switch to an OCD specialist.
I feel a kind of peace with that knowledge.
I want to thank you for your advice.
I'm a titanic father.
My only private pleasure is gathering seashells.
People like that should all die.

DAY 86

I need strength for when you're not here.
Deferring decisions always has bad consequences.
I can do anything here; the work is all on you.
Everything had to be quote unquote important.
You can crush me with your steamroller.
I don't know how to get out there with you.
She's just a happy and disoriented person.
So much has been taken from me.
I would love to show people this thing.
It's not as bad as you're making it seem.
Now you'll say we'll just have to see.

DAY 87

I don't trust my own words; only yours.
That's very helpful, when you put it like that.
So what am I supposed to do with that?
Look at me, see, I dress in neon.
Do you actually like me?
The only desire I have is for perfection.
They could speak of real, adult, male experience—
amazing.
I did what you said, moved on.
I am committed to this, in my way.
That's pretty obvious, isn't it?

DAY 88

You could always say it's me who's failing.
My nighttime experience is worsening.

DAY 89

Maybe I should spend all my time in Nature.
It was the most ridiculous display of female flesh.
It's so hot that he's a "ladies man".
Who cares about gravy dropping on the table cloth?
Too fast or too slow—either way I'm wrong.
The phone call ends and I'm abandoned again.
No child should speak to her father like she speaks to me.
And now I have you.
I just want you to have the full picture.

DAY 90

I can't tell if I was an idiot or a hero.
You can't fuck with me, I said to my daughter.
Mommy picked a bad idea.
Saying I hate my wife doesn't make me feel good.
Nothing I say to you ever makes sense.
I never worry about how smart I am.
If you try, you die.

DAY 91

It would be easier if my mother were a crackhead.
Talking to you places me at the center of a panorama.
I'm interested in these very small windows.
I know what you'll say if I call it stupid.
I want to see you but not see myself.
I want you to validate what I'm saying.

DAY 92

I feel dead, no more gloss or glitter.
I always go back to regret.
Hating my wife is part of being alive.
You just made me feel understood.
I have an identity only if I do what I should.
I have never been a misogynist.
I'd have to be insane to sign on to that.
I feel so fried by my mother.

DAY 93

I'm moved by you but then what?
That's really helpful.
People shit on me and no one apologizes.
Please listen to me.
What if you and I don't go slowly?
I don't usually bring these feelings out.
I'm getting too clumsy in the metaphor.

DAY 94

Meaning vanishes when I think you're not listening.
I'm leaning in to the tailspin.

DAY 95

I keep allowing myself to be stressed.
I need to do it better than anyone.
I think you're being naive.
What do you mean by an authentic son?
I don't think of myself as having a personality.
It's not about keeping you away.
That would be the most painful thing you could do to me.

DAY 96

I can't stand the word "love".
I don't have the right to be sad.
Speaking to you is me taking the time and effort.
I can't accept what I know is true.
It's so fucking scary to say these things.
I can keep myself invisible on the screen.
That's exactly what I was going to say.

DAY 97

Power always corrupts me.
I'm scared of what I would do with weapons.
He shoved a wad of toilet paper down my throat.
I will hurt people if I'm free.
I don't want to stay closed like this.
I don't have to worry about overburdening you.
The right person could put him out to pasture.

DAY 98

"I don't know" means I don't commit.
Wanting to be an adult is being an adult.
That's just you being a guy.
I hate yearning for structure.
What you're saying is I'm doomed and fucked.
My association is to Otto Rank.
I don't know if I want to be myself.
You're watching for my speaking errors.

DAY 99

"Himself" is the only real person.
Being a thug is exciting.
I need us to be on the same team.

DAY 100

A greater thinker would be better at this than we are.
How do people carry on when I feel so nervous?
My kids are just like, not good.
I feel so fragile getting ready to talk with you.
All you say—I see it, agree with it, know it, and don't
know what to do with it.
I cry when it feels like you can see me.
No one deserves my sneering.
It was magical and this isn't.
Don't start; don't get going.

DAY 101

Are you there or are you doing something else?
I assure you I'm getting something from these sessions.
I hope you've received my payment.
I swear I didn't want her to become attracted to me.
Sometimes you're really good at advice.
I'm great being a father.
I feel confused by the state of the world.

DAY 102

It seems like weeks since we spoke.
Nothing I say now would make you happy.
Maybe the show trial will end by tomorrow.
I never thought of it that way, but, yeah.
A bickering Jewish couple—I'm living my nightmare.
I leapfrogged what you just said.
It's complicated, staying safe.
Talking like an idiot is much worse than living like one.
Death is the master.

DAY 103

I envy how intensely she lives.
No, it's not discipline, it's self-regulation.
On what planet do you think I fucking owe you anything?
I don't have the right to speak about myself to you.
I need you to give me permission to sulk.
How do I stop being a jerk to my parents, Don?
Please just hear me out.
I did all the things a normal human being would do.

DAY 104

That makes me feel this is a purely financial transaction.
I need to write down the things you say.
I'm so excited that I can remake the entire world.
I only feel good when I make her feel bad.
I don't even try to remember our sessions.
That's what I meant by anxious attachment.
Is that a new haircut, new glasses?
I think you could sense the upcoming explosion.

DAY 105

Can breath work supplement what we do?
You're too much of a communist to get this.
I'm managing this and her friends are not.
This is no time to be talking to my therapist.
Do you think I'm going too fast?
You might say that all of that was useless.

DAY 106

Some people do take care of others.
I was ranked and then—no offer.
I don't want to use my family as things.
It's so steep that I might need to walk.
I don't know how to hold on to you.
My room is organized the way I like it organized.
This guy's fucked; what a miserable way to live.
I totally understand if you bill me for the session.
I do really good work and then get stoned for three days.
I panicked when you asked me what I meant.
You're so fucking severe.

DAY 107

This is a reasonably excellent outcome.
Lockdown exposes how irreversible your choices are.
You fell for someone even more fucked-up than I am.
As the only one, I'm either zero or crazy.
I feel like a failure, always.
It would be easier to pay you later.
I'll tattoo "Unhappy Man" on my arm.
Everyone I know is a fucking, rock'n'roll drug user.

DAY 108

10,000 photos—I must have had an interesting life.
I go blank when you ask a question.
I have to defend my brother against what you say.
I feel deserted and abandoned when the kids leave.
I want to forget everything—that's not so bad.
What were your insights from last week?
I'm not like a broken robot who can't do this.
It takes work to resist her wiles.
I'm representing my interests and the safety of our child.

DAY 109

Whatever I say can't be taken back.
What if I never meet anyone else?
I want to leave indelible phrases behind.
It's not really confusing, to be honest, it's frustrating.
I am not an abusive person.
Let's bet about tomorrow's session.

DAY 110

I can't even imagine a dialogue, you there and me here.
I want to be a good guy who helps her get through this.
I have to go; text me some times.
That would make me kind of a bad person.
I believe you won't forget me and I don't.
I'm the killer father and the son he wants to kill.
Yes, of course, this is what we need to do.
The present tense is clumsy and ungainly.

DAY 111

Being in the flow is not sustainable, is it?
I like that phrase, saving you from yourself.
We've been over this so many times already.
Whatever, and the reasons aren't interesting.
You want to take everything I have.
I admire you for coming up with that metaphor.
I asked my daughter: "what's it like being you?"
I do good things only by accident.
Am I ever allowed to be simply simple?

DAY 112

Being so angry makes me feel clear-headed.
A spread sheet gives you a giant block of your whole life.
I feel for you but I feel for me too.
I want to hide under the covers.
He erased me so I erased myself.
What is the relevance of money?
My dad hates blue heron.
I can't see the shape of my life.
I'm really afraid.

DAY 113

Danger comes the moment my life is mine.
I want to get a knife and stab him in the neck.
I don't want to convey the impression that I'm anxious.
At times I've called my childhood perfect.
I called prostitutes but didn't do anything.
What you just said sounds right on.

DAY 114

I reach but I can't find myself.
Under pressure I turn into a child.
Jews would have let Hitler kill all the Poles.
I should have never been born.
I want to do violence to that person.
Maybe I do have a lot to be angry about.
That would be patronizing and paternalistic.
You sound judgmental even if you're not.
My headphones weren't connected so I hung up anyway.
I'm desperately rooting for shit again.

DAY 115

We're all going to die; it's way too dangerous.
Funny how analysis can make you feel hungry
afterwards.
These fucking peasants don't deserve me.
I'm sorry about screwing up the time.
I got hard but it's silly to talk about.
I've told you all my problems; now what?
I'm like a cheerleader with pom-poms.
I don't think you meant that as a prescription.

DAY 116

I'm just keeping this conversation going until the time
comes.
You don't say "Hi, how are you?"
My violent mob rule impulse makes me uncomfortable.
I'm stuck on that, the importance of physical
attractiveness.
I felt so relaxed and comforted by her.
I can think with you but nowhere else.
I don't want to feel that way for weeks.
That fits in with the propositions we're working on.

DAY 117

I had a companion inside of me and then it was gone.
This is not 19th century Kazakhstan.
People do reach out to me.
Why can't I relish the scotch and the leather chair?
I felt energized after taking the poison and vomiting,
vomiting, vomiting.
I'm really afraid of what the cocaine will do to me.
If I can get myself excited, I'd take this seriously.

DAY 118

I'm not allowed to focus on love until I've figured out
money.
We're affectionate but only when we go to resorts.
This country breaks my heart.
What kind of father doesn't love his daughters?
You were repairing my laptop and giving me food.
That is very well said.
You'll hang up the phone and never speak to me.
If this is digressing, just let me know.
I'm drinking, eating, and pulling the hair on my chin.

DAY 119

I am pretty divided myself.
It's purposeful well-styled aggressiveness.
At the end of the day, you're just another bitch.
It moves my body toward heart palpitations.
It's not what I thought I'd be talking about.
I'm amazed how much I'm fantasizing about coupling.
I'll just retreat to family and friends.
It's a kind of Hail Mary on my part.
After we speak, I need to get out a notebook.

DAY 120

I regret whatever I do.
I don't feel very authentic around them.
All that civilization and maybe I'm a violent sadist.
This really exposes a darkness inside myself.
How can I feel less lonely and unloved?
So, my mother is sick now for the past five days.
You say it's ours but really you mean it's yours.

DAY 121

Your saying resentment really got to me.
Breath work really opens me up.
But you've seen this before in me, right?
I hate this country.
Every mistake is a major mistake.
I can feel my redemption slipping away.

DAY 122

What I want is for someone to know me.
I treat my life like an emergency situation.
I cancelled because I was just hating myself too much.
There is no difference between punishment and reward.
I want to start with where we ended.
That can't be who she really is.
My mother may outlive me.

DAY 123

I may be making up everything I say about myself.
I was too nice, not aggressive enough.
What crime have I committed?
I'm going to have to write while feeling scared.
I don't have anything for you today.
I know you're trying to guide me somewhere.
You become like who you're with.
And then I instantly implicate myself.
I don't learn.

DAY 124

Sobbing like that was like vomiting.
I like seeing you on Zoom.
It's always just a matter of inches.
I'm really bitter.
It's not just you, I want everyone to feel sorry for me.
When I was five, I made a little bowel movement in class.
I never used to think I was an anxious person.
I like your long speeches.
I'm in a state of denial.
Swinging between two poles—that's my equilibrium.
Harder, harder, closer, don't forgive—that's you,
Dr. Conscience.

DAY 125

Who would ever want to have a child with me?
Now I have a group.
She says I'm a tentacled monster.
Now there are three women interested in me.
Like you said, it's a very inefficient way of maintaining
equilibrium.
The perfect scores don't count; only the failures do.
The only way out is by magic.

DAY 126

I couldn't really understand your writing.
So, Los Angeles is a lie, right?
Yes, my father was a good guy.
I tried to make my son feel guilty.
I don't really believe anything I say.
I thought I would read this to you.
My social life revolves around drug use.
I never wanted to become an adult man.

DAY 127

I don't know how to talk with you when my mind is just drifting.
People don't know who I am or why I'm there.
It's great that you're willing to meet me halfway.
You can't really blame it on me.
People are taken aback when I'm angry.
It's this wounded-to-be-superior thing.
You had a good insight a couple weeks ago.
I can't imagine an interested audience.

DAY 128

What do you mean when you say "cloudy"?
What I want is deeper than understanding.
I don't know where to go forward to.
One thing is knowing it, another is to cope with it.
My emails have always been too long.
There was no freedom to be me.
I'm going over my notes from last time.
I encounter reality and hang my head in my hands.
You only treat disaffected privileged white men like myself.
We're selling our house.

DAY 129

I was feeling so recharged but woke up in enormous pain.
I'm sick of being in the middle: I want to land.
Did your kids go into therapy?
It's not the whole solution but still just do it.
My mom went deep into religion.
God damn it, let me finish.
I almost ordered cocaine.

DAY 130

The man couldn't speak after what he had seen.
Oh, it's OK, I can just die alone.
I'll stitch it together for you.
I can't remember when we spoke last.
I'll think about who I am and tell you next time.
I don't trust you either.
I can't ask you to ask me a question.
I'm trapped back in my childhood.
The logical conclusion is to double down.
I put my head against her bosom.
There's a refusal to do that.

DAY 131

She's not stupid; she just has stupid ideas.
It's all "we" this and "we" that.
There's a strong desire to be almost virginal.
What's at the bottom?
Skiing has something to do with death.
I have an aversion to her being ordinary and lackluster.
Whether it's the money or the uncooked chicken, it's
challenging.
Everything I'm doing is for my father.
I'm crying now.
What do I get from talking about this?

DAY 132

I have been conditioned to hold onto this stuff.
I can't tell whether my needs are excessive.
I wanted to get something accomplished with you.
My mother wants me in on her most private secret.
If that's true, why shouldn't I just kill myself?
I feel the need for constant validation.

DAY 133

She offered me everything she had—$57.
Our Christmas plans are falling apart.
I don't mean to say my relationships to my children are
trivial.
I'm making myself, intentionally or otherwise, imperfect.
Am I right or am I worthless?
I kind of feel activated at the moment.
I need to get going with the rest of my life.
There's a secret here and a lie there.
You intimidate me.

DAY 134

Nobody here drives pickup trucks.
There's a sexual element with my mother.
My mother says I'm a piece of shit.
Why bother even asking?
I don't know why I'm not worth it.
Reassurance is like food when you're hungry.
I'll see you in my dreams.
I don't trust you: I trust my kids.
Every way I say it is not what I mean to say.

DAY 135

I want to find an esoteric interpretation for this.
It's so nice to be around all that innocent energy.
For the first time, I'm lonely in New York.
Being uninvited is a huge warning sign.
How can I possibly love the man I am?
There has been some sort of correctable mistake.
People's minds are being radically altered.
I'm stewing in these ideas, but nothing moves.
I had a profound connection to my mother.

DAY 136

I'm forgetting these things I wouldn't normally forget.
That was the first time he behaved like a man.
Writing her obituary tipped me over.
I should already be where I hope to be.
I really don't know what I'm doing here.

DAY 137

It was just a totalizing fear.
She's beautiful so I'm attractive.
She says I'm emotionally abusive.
I pretend I'm in control of the chaos.
I'm looking for tranquility in San Diego.
I need these problems in order to survive.
It's a lot easier to speak about pain.
I've been toying with envy and resentment.
Weakness turns me into a fucking bitch.

DAY 138

I really don't like this.
I really hate putting on pounds.
I want more than rational caring from you.
I deserved every indulgence.
I should sit in my corner and shut up.
I would be worthy of their love.
I want our children to be independent.
The thinking itself is different.

DAY 139

We're in a circle and I won't keep doing it.
I don't feel like rested and energized.
What is known is the self-destructiveness of it.
I try to fill the work slot.
I don't have anyone to jump to.
I'm just waiting for the time to pass here.
She put a cork in it.
She'll become a different person.
My body is wet meat with hair and fingernails attached.

DAY 140

I feel cared for in restaurants.
It's an endless pile of plastic crap.
The work is a refuge from the pain.
The boundaries began to slip a bit.
Look at us: just two guys on the phone.
Video games are an intuitive solution.
I understand if you won't give me advice.

DAY 141

I wish I could access a self-portrait for you.
I'm trying to remember what you look like.
I should deal with my own issues.
I was really rattled by our last session.
I have never known what I want.
It makes me feel like a failed man.
I'm waiting for a make-believe thing.
There's not enough emotion to go around.
Is this Invasion of the Body Snatchers?
I want attention paid to my book.

DAY 142

My gyroscope has me always pointed toward her.
I imagine you angry and snapping.
You've been late sometimes as well.
Really, I have to pay for your retardation?
Don't throw the word "difficult" down my throat.

DAY 143

I feel like this whole thing is not going to end well.
It starts in my body, like a weight on my chest.
I think I'm going surfing this weekend.
I'm terrified that the world will go away.
I need to figure how to get out of jail.
I'm encased in a cabinet of my own thoughts.
This is my first experience of real solitude.
I realize how dug in that harshness is.
You pressure me to read what's hurtful.

DAY 144

Someone else would have fought back.
I'm cursed: I'll never get what I want.
I don't think I'm a raging hypochondriac.
Sometimes I just want a hug from my mother.
Your word, "complicity", really hit me.

DAY 145

Is it possible to not be dehumanized?
It's related to addiction, but not really.
I offload my stress onto you.
We skirt around the sexual stuff.
I like your term, "money men".
I don't know if I can do this.
I never had casual, a lot of casual.
I'm vibrating at a certain frequency.
I didn't want to be in the world anymore.
Now is not the time for honesty.

DAY 146

I'm letting you down.
You and I are both decent guys.
I have no interest in safe, reliable men.
I have to get at something deeper.
Neither of us is ever aggressive here.
My mom pushes these men on me.
I did cocaine last night.
The closer we get, the less intimate I feel.

DAY 147

I need to set myself in motion.
I'm trying to not give a fuck.
I am always anxious with my kids.
Jews in my family love Christmas.
I don't know who Donald Moss is.
It's probably all on me.
You always write about bitter experience.
You can help me find myself.
Staying dead is a reliable form of stability.
I don't want my dad as a financial overlord.
Terror is the word that comes to mind.

DAY 148

You have to stay three steps ahead, not just one.
My body responds immediately to my will.
We're primitive dark borderline people.
There's an aesthetic to heroin.
Why did you ask what I wanted from you?
I should be in the position to help my dad.

DAY 149

I want a decision without consequences.
We were in the same room but couldn't connect.
She said you were the most brilliant man.

DAY 150

I reduce myself to the role of extra.
I'm trying to think of an actual example for you.
Almost escaping is so sad.
Death is what's waiting for me.
I want to be better at living.
I just haven't found the right way.
I'm trying to understand idealization.
I get pissed off whenever you say that.
What if I use the treatment against myself?
My wife and I got into an enormous fight again.

DAY 151

There's no audience to remind me that I'm separate.
I want an extended break from our sessions.
That's exactly what I want: convenience.
I don't know why I'm irritable today.
Finally, a sense of steady incremental progress.
I've gotten away with not working my whole life.

DAY 152

There's only space for one: hopeful or hopeless.
You actually have a lot of influence over me.
But how do we deal with abandonment for our next session?
It's only OK if I am the violent one.
The baby is a vortex asking for attention.
I'm afraid of saying anything to you.
My mom doesn't speak about the hardships.
I can only talk to my dad, not to you.

DAY 153

No point in thinking about deeply ingrained habits.
If I were Black, this would make me very angry.
Dr. Moss, how should this be structured?
I would like to have one human that cares about me.
Good news: it's not an STD.
I've got nothing.
I'm helpless with desire.
I just know that people are temporary.
I'm just trying to get access to my money.

DAY 154

Am I cool, am I a loser, am I unnecessary?
Have you read the book, "How to Change Your Mind?"
I am so grateful to be feeling again.
I am not vicious; I'm kind.
Won't you grant that some things are beyond agency?
If I'm alone, it's no longer luck; it's failure.
I want you to tell me what to do.
I want a human relationship with my parents.
I don't want to talk to you about anything.

DAY 155

I'm not sure how speaking with you will matter.
I'm afraid you won't think I'm intelligent.
She has lawsuits and physical therapy—basically nothing.
I'm really down on myself, even after hitting every
deadline.
I want to use all my contacts before they get dusty.
Everything is just down, down, down.
I'm trying to speak with you seriously.
I'm harder to provoke.
I never, never, never even try.

DAY 156

I met some girls so I'm feeling much better.
Did I tell you about the insurance bill?
Seeing a Black person, the n-word comes into my head.
You can tell me I don't deserve to be happy.
I don't know how to detach from my childhood.
45 minutes of work and then I say "I'm good".
She's a chaos fairy.
I've never felt connected to anyone.
You could tell her I'm a dumb idiot.

DAY 157

I just want to be great at something.
I'm locked in, as though in a bathtub.
The abuse was out of desperation, not animal force.
If for some godforsaken reason I forget, will you just text me?
I have no hesitation saying there's been progress here.
You might be getting frustrated with me.
I've put my hat in the ring.
Maybe we need more sessions.
I'm entirely sick of lockdown at this point.

DAY 158

There should be urgency but there isn't.
Deep down, I can't be loved.
I've always had a lot of boyfriends.
She's basically kind of racist.
We did talking and kissing.
It's OK to feel superior as long as people don't know it.
How do you think I should deal with my son?
I just want someone to tell me what to do.
I shouldn't have done it, but …

DAY 159

With women, I'm not part of the bond between them.
You're not allowed to think highly of yourself.
I feel grateful to you for our last session.
We'll see if you'll love me in five minutes.
I always wondered if my mom would abandon me.

DAY 160

I'm not a baby—I can take it.
I couldn't do it—several weeks in an ocean storm.
He scoffed at me whenever I wanted help.
She always slapped the spoon from her mouth.
At least I can punish myself now.
I need to see at least some light ahead of me.
Someone please give me a fucking clue.
I'm not going to assert my dominance over anyone.
She just doesn't seem attuned.

DAY 161

I fill my notebook with hexagonal symmetries.
It's not the beginning of decay and disorder.
Your face is smooth, like you've come through
something.
What time do we end today?
I don't get off by beating myself up.
There are always power imbalances.
You didn't mean it, but I still felt shamed.
Don't talk to addicts when they're all fucked up.
My thoughts are like tadpoles.
It's either perfect or worthless.

DAY 162

It was a funny day yesterday—we got married.
I'm running out of magical solutions.
I don't feel comfortable talking to you about woman
things.
If I can't connect it to childhood, then I can't be free.
You're leaving me hanging on a string.
Only men should be taken seriously.
It seems like I'm doing ok, right?
I want to be separate, alone.
Just looking for a simulacrum of companionship.

DAY 163

I was afraid that would make you angry.
I need to protect you from feeling fragile or weak.
Oh God, I thought I got rid of him.
If I'm powerful, I get afraid of being mad.
I'm a submarine and you're a fish.
It no-sex started when she got pregnant.
How many patients do you actually have?
Stronger and more virile but nothing to do with it.
My environment may be affecting me.

DAY 164

I want to cry at the complexity of it.
It depends what you mean by cloudy.
I can never be happy.
In my head it's what I'm supposed to do.
You're good at making me feel stupid.
I'm imagining someone looking at me and telling me I
can do it.
I'm not manic-depressive.
It was an explicitly extreme orgiastic setting.

DAY 165

They can only get help over the phone.
Dr. Moss has become impatient with me.
I want to give that cookbook to my father.
Everything and everyone is a threat.
That sounds almost right.
It just makes me feel stupid.

DAY 166

I sit in her window and look at the snow.
I don't answer the questions I ask.
No one can stand hearing about sexual abuse.
Our brains meld; we're perfectly synced.
I'm already tired of hearing my own voice.
I feel superior and inferior.
What else is there to talk about?
This level of isolation—it's really not healthy.

DAY 167

My hand still hurts from banging the walls.
My main emotion these days is anger or sadness.
It's so grey, so winter.
I don't really have much choice in the matter.
I was able to put every element together.
This may be skin cancer.
I'm becoming more curious.
I'm afraid of arguing with you.

DAY 168

Sixteen months is kind of a long time.
I don't mean to sound so petty.
I'm in no hurry to stop.
I have to be engaged, topical and political.
I don't believe in the god I need.
You set a standard of acceptance that I can't meet.
I don't have skin cancer, but I still feel the same.
They were steps on my ascension.
Maybe I should just read this to you.
Come back home and, whoa, it's real.

DAY 169

I'm lying and cheating wherever I go.
I'm at least a decent storyteller.
Everything goes directly into my body.
Maybe it's better to be depressed than angry.
I'm ashamed I'm heteronormative.
You would be crazy if you actually did that.
I'm worried about the observers.
The point is to feel good about yourself.
I get grounded by not feeling anxious.

DAY 170

What is there that's hard to talk about?
She wants me to be honest about everything.
I waffle between petrified and unstable.
My daughter says her therapist casts a spell on her.
Think it's wrong or stupid to take medication?
Where does all my violence come from?
I don't have access to what you want from me.
That's how I would be if I were alive.
Fuck my history.

DAY 171

I want to ask you how you are, where you're from.
How far can I go without becoming mad?
I just don't have the patience for her.
I feel sad now, a tightness in my chest.
I'm smart, people like me and I'm reasonably
good-looking.
The lack of touch is unbearable.
Rabbits don't even eat carrots.
Eight hours of Twitter since yesterday's session.

DAY 172

People will be jealous if I take pleasure in my work.
Yesterday's session is already old news.
I don't blame them, really, to be honest with you.
I'm just a fucking idiot.
Proving I'm good actually proves I'm bad.
Being neglected is unbearable.
I join the enemy.
I'm depleted the next day.
Moss is thinking who is this guy.

DAY 173

Can you hear the waves in the background?
Moss will give me what I need over the counter.
Therapy interferes with being Superwoman.
Have you ever been to Key West?
I hate being called "Daddy".
I haven't really accepted that my marriage is over.
I don't have the discipline for grief.

DAY 174

What do you think that is?
How do you stop twisting it into yourself?
The only true things are negative.
You've certainly heard all of this before.
How would you define my sexuality?
I can't even put on a condom right.
We were going to be good for each other.
I'm thinking of doing real harm to myself.
You're the grey-haired wizard.

DAY 175

Don't tell me what I already know.
How can you be such a fucking moron?
I don't know why I'm in a bad mood.
I'm feeling a heavy weight now.
I'm so tired of being set up for failure.
I've stopped brushing my teeth.
Are you writing a book or something?
I don't sound like I'm taking this seriously.

DAY 176

I want to create a beautiful interior space.
I don't mean to sound arrogant.
Every morning I wake up scared.
I'm actually proud that I haven't hurt myself.
Is it OK to feel superior?
We cannot decide what is really important.
I can't survive another episode like that.
How do captains of industry deal with their concerns?
I am not a criminal.
My judgment on that was not compromised.

DAY 177

I didn't like her but she did have very beautiful hair.
She's not the person you would give your jewelry to.
I can feel my body softening when you speak.
Lying doesn't make him a bad person.
There's no possibility of innocence.
I don't know who I'm talking to at all.
I'm holding on to zero.
First graders are making cupcakes for Black people.
What am I waiting for?
None of what I'm saying matters.

DAY 178

No need for her to lie to me anymore.
There was no impulse to cause pain.
Music is such a powerful way to remember.
I can whip people into reality distortion.
That's my dog drinking from the toilet.
She'd tell everyone how fucked-up I was.
Any kind of assertion is a problem.
It was perfect—our son on her lap.
I don't want to see things that way.
I am not OK.

DAY 179

I am afraid to come out of the shadows.
These bills are fucking frightening.
I'm better today; I'm fine.
It's a positive self-negation.
If I wash more dishes, maybe she'll sleep with me.
I should have started with this.
I don't want catastrophic destruction.

DAY 180

I want to squash and conquer her independence.
I don't want to blame my mother.
Yesterday I completely admired myself.
If it's right in front of my eyeballs, I can do it.
I want you to love and take care of me.
Can I handle him as a billionaire celebrity?
I say OK to every demand.

DAY 181

None of the people I'm with is magical.
I'm extremely productive and feeling great.
But I am afraid to remember what he did to me.
Pain keeps me connected to him.
I feel ashamed of my hackneyed desire.
I apologize.
That will be the beginning of the end.
I was the only white guy on the street.

DAY 182

It doesn't matter if it's not true.
The only way to show hatred is to leave.
Most people think abuse is a one-way thing.
I have to put up with my tedious kids.
I sit on the chair lift and there's nothing inside.
I only start crying when I'm talking to you.
Fuck you, man!
They're trying to gaslight me.

DAY 183

With the men, there are no decisions to make.
It's pain and anger I'm after.
He's interesting and I'm interested.
There's a lot of stress in the car.
I help them work through their feelings.
That's where my father seems to reappear.
It's a revolt against being left alone.
I don't want any of this.
I want to meet regular people.
It didn't work out with that girl.

DAY 184

I'm the one who's having fun.
From 5th grade on, I had no one to turn to.
I don't know what I'm being accused of.
I don't take responsibility for being alive.
In role play, I am the character who can see things.
I'm not going to stop having money.
I want to be home and never leave.
Life is shit.
I can't plan more than six seconds ahead.
You staying still is intimidating.

DAY 185

She was bat-shit crazy.
Surgeons and pilots cannot lose anything.
There is no one to protect me.
I learned what you learn by reading a book.
There is a chip on my shoulder.
I am just so angry.
What is it like for you to write?
You are warmer than my previous therapist.
I am not aware of what's going on here.

DAY 186

I once allowed my father to see me naked.
I'd rather be cold than be enraged like that.
I would just turn into a maniac.
That's it?
Do you happen to know a writing coach?
I was asked to do it myself.
My real intention is to just get away.
I spent Saturday stoned.
I feel she is a Satanic person.

DAY 187

I'm only being defensive when I am cold and distant.
I'm back here after eight years away.
I'm giving up on feeling any good.
I smoke to get away from everyone.
I couldn't stay in role.
I'm slowly picking up these tools of normalcy.

DAY 188

Why am I so afraid to be alone?
You're good but you're not so great.
We're afraid of the con-demic.
I've finally made a friend.
I was trusting a fucking sociopath.
You're treating me with a secret plan.
I am not a video artist.

DAY 189

I'm always looking to relax my brain.
Since yesterday, I've begun to feel adrift, incoherent.
I'm in a cage I can't dismantle.
The problem is I'm not a scumbag.
I am pitiless.
Odysseus at least didn't hate himself.
My father casts a very big shadow.
I've absolved myself of doing any work.
Can't I just nap?
You could write me off as a hopeless case.
I want to say I overcame the anxiety around …

LIST OF FIRST LINES

Lightning Source UK Ltd.
Milton Keynes UK
UKHW022223010822
406706UK00010B/89